Beware of the Dragon

Written by Gemma Bagnall

Illustrated by Eva Morales

It was Friday afternoon, and Miss Aman couldn't wait to show the children her box of stories.

"What will you pick?" she asked Tam.

"I know!" cried Tam, pulling some shimmering green fabric from the box. "We could tell a dragon story!"

"I can't wait to hear it," said Miss Aman.

Tam, Bella-Rose and Billy spent the rest of the day fighting off the dragon.

After school, they carried on at Tam's house.

They fended off the dragon's gnashing jaws with shields and helmets of shining silver.

They hid on their knees behind a huge rock, to dodge the dragon's burning flames.

"Oh no!" called Bella-Rose. "The dragon got Billy – and now he's stuck at the top of the tower!"

"We must save him!" said Tam, grabbing the shield.

Bella-Rose and Tam began to climb, ducking to avoid getting burnt.

"Don't let the dragon get you!" called Billy. "It will gobble you up!"

"Dragons don't scare me!" replied Bella-Rose, still climbing.

When they got to the top, Bella-Rose and Tam set Billy free.

"You're safe," they said.

Just then, they heard a low rumble from the bottom of the tower.

The dragon had fallen asleep!

"Let's go," said Billy. "Don't put a foot wrong or you'll wake it!"

The children crept past the sleeping dragon.

Suddenly, there was
a loud **DING DONG!**

"Bella-Rose and Billy! Time to go home!" called Tam's dad.

The children froze, their eyes on the dragon. Would it wake up?

The dragon was still.

The children let out a sigh of relief.

"Thank goodness you didn't wake the dragon!" said Billy.

"You lot are full of stories," said Tam's dad, chuckling as he folded the sleeping dragon away.